Cold Remembered
and other poems

by

David R. Altman

Finishing Line Press
Georgetown, Kentucky

Cold Remembered
and other poems

For Lisa, with love

Copyright © 2023 by David R. Altman
ISBN 979-8-88838-110-6 First Edition
All rights reserved under International and Pan-American Copyright Conventions. No part of this book may be reproduced in any manner whatsoever without written permission from the publisher, except in the case of brief quotations embodied in critical articles and reviews.

ACKNOWLEDGMENTS

Some of these poems first appeared in these publications:

American Journal of Poetry, "Picking Up My Crying Father at the Airport", July 2017
Blue Mountain Review, "Turning Away from Sarah McLachlan," December 2017
Finishing Line Press, "Death in the Foyer", October 2014
Riza Press, "Cold Remembered", *Multimedia Poetry and Art Journal*, January 2020

I want to thank my family for their love and support. Lisa, Jennifer, Katie & Ashley—I love you guys. And for the love and support of my late parents, Bob and Donna Altman and for the love of the world's greatest aunt, Gloria Davis of Hilliard, Ohio. I am also grateful for the wisdom inspiration and influence of David Bottoms and Will Wright—both as teachers and as gifted poets. Finally, a special thanks to my dear friend and fellow poet Dub Taft, for his support, encouragement and friendship.

Publisher: Leah Huete de Maines
Editor: Christen Kincaid
Cover Art: Taken of the author at Lake of the Woods, Baudette, Minnesota January 2001, by the late Kevin Marchuk, Rainy River, Ontario ("Go Leafs")
Author Photo: Katie McWhorter
Cover Design: Ashley A. Salyer

Order online: www.finishinglinepress.com
also available on amazon.com

Author inquiries and mail orders:
Finishing Line Press
PO Box 1626
Georgetown, Kentucky 40324
USA

Table of Contents

Early Memories
Picking Up My Crying Father at the Airport 1
Beyond the Carcass 2
Cold Remembered 3
Morning Song 4

Seasons
Who's in Charge Here? 7
What She Would Have Wanted 9
When Time Is Up 10

Love Unknown
Memory Lane 13
First Step 14
Drawing Near 15
Waiting for Isabelle 16
Deprivation 17
Confessions 18

Passages
Dream Weavers 21
Twelve Fingered Saints 22
Death in the Foyer 23
Speed Bumps 24

Summer Evenings
Turning Away from Sarah McLachlan 27
Guard Duty 29
Who is Listening? 30
The Whistler 31

Early Memories

"Good and bad, I define these terms
Quite clear, no doubt, somehow
Ah but I was so much older then,
I'm younger than that now."
—Bob Dylan, "My Back Pages"

Picking Up My Crying Father at the Airport

1.

Never had I watched or created
A scene so memorable as when my father
Sat crying at the airport curb, his ears filled with bloody cotton,
My brother and I watched, more curious than scared,
Our mother helping him into the car.

2.

The flurries fell as slowly as the silent
Businessmen who quietly passed my
Injured father like the woman who knew CPR but rode past the man collapsed
behind his lawnmower, because, well, the ambulance would be there soon.
There was no interest, no time to stop for a crying
Middle-aged man who had just lost
His hearing.

3.

Inside the car, my father leaned forward, heavy against the dashboard,
Holding his ears, my mother, upright and frightened to drive at night,
Holding her tears, like the brave child, chin up, before the injection,
She drives down the icy airport ramp,
Unable to respond to the questions that came
From the back seat.

4.

My father's crying stopped but his hearing never returned.
A plane bound from Chicago to Columbus depressurized
At 28,000 feet, cruelly propelling
His eardrums toward the stars—an uncommon occurrence
For an uncommon man.

Beyond the Carcass

The deer carcass curled
about the tree, unattended
and unseen except
by those that passed its withering,
coyotes had roared into their hunger
and snagged all the deer's life away,
but the hide was left intact.
like a burlap sack draped over bones.

When I pass roadkill,
I fixate on the blooms that flourish
behind their decay
that seem to form a petaled radiance
around the dead.

Cold Remembered

1.

As a child
my parents wrapped my toes
with aluminum foil scavenged
from stadium hamburgers
to prevent frostbite
at a Cleveland Browns game.

2.

I have known cold
as no one else.
I have pissed
into wind at minus forty
when the ice was six feet thick
on Lake of the Woods.
Then, returning to the ice
shack, still filled
with Labatt's Blue, lying beside
the burning reefer and the frozen walleye.

3.

I could feel myself starting to slip
across the boat's stern.
the recently waxed
surface created a violent,
unstoppable ride, flailing
arms, nothing to grab hold of,
my friend's arm reaching too late.
I disappeared into the frigid water,
the last I saw of myself
in the eyes of my drowning brother.

Morning Song

There's something moving on my deck
it's still too dark to see.
at once the Towhee sings her song,
a cup of breakfast tea.

She looks as though she wants to nest
her partner turns his head,
last year's nest has come and gone,
it's back to work instead.

The Towhee's song has just one verse
it echoes through the trees,
Carolina Wrens soon join in,
a symphony tunes its keys.

The Cardinal's chirp a snare drum's beat
to Piliated's jungle cry,
Chickadees line up to whistle,
the Red Tail circles high.

The warming sun completes the scene
as morning's chorus soon will fade,
the trees will hold their songs for now,
a refuge in the shade.

Seasons

Lord, let me die   but not die
Out.
—James Dickey, "The Last Wolverine"

Who's in Charge Here?

Her voice and eyes seemed broken now
still waiting for the cure,
We strained to listen as she spoke,
the grace of pain she must endure.

The lawn needs mowing though it must wait
for someone else to give,
Kindness of a different sort
that lets us all forgive.

As there is nothing man can do
that faith has not already done,
Keeping family close and true,
a binding strength for father-son.

We keep our distance as we were taught
and give the ill the room they need,
But distance just prolongs the plot,
of jilted nerves, a prayer for speed.

She fights the fight we know too well
against the fiercest foe,
The days grow shorter, a longer hell,
A tent without a show.

People shop in grocery stores
while pic lines soon come out,
Life to most is open doors,
except for those who favor doubt.

The littlest one will lift her now,
she smiles against the tears,
Peace that comes with renewed vows,
to fight the pain; to lift the fears.

The hardest lesson to receive,
from those who will not give,
The smallest hope, the last reprieve,
a chance that they will live.

What She Would Have Wanted
for C.D.

"It's what she would have wanted,"
Said the family as she laid,
As hospice nurses move undaunted,
From morphine to the grave.

To have a chance to go back home
"It's what she would have wanted"
Her sons and husband stand alone,
Now escorts unconfronted.

Decisions made by her alone,
No second guesses drawn,
No angel escort to the throne,
No faith to face the dawn.

With springtime blooms the hospice room's
A closet nearly haunted,
With backwards glance, the living say
"It's what she would have wanted."

When Time Is Up

When time is up and all is well,
she could feel the evening swell
Against a doubled life of hell,
a fate she sensed she could not quell.

Come quickly, now, and don't cry out,
to those you follow you must not shout,
The love of times no one would doubt,
a danger zone you cannot tout.

Free them now and let them stir,
those memories that did comfort her,
Of times so rich that made her stir,
uncertain cries of things unsure.

At last she left without a song,
it left her as the leaves were gone,
The heart she left was always strong,
the ones she left must now belong.

Love Unknown

Parting is all we know of heaven and all we need of hell.
—Emily Dickinson, "My Life Closed Twice Before Its Close"

Memory Lane

She rode among the chicken houses,
her horse slogging uphill, downwind of the chickens
but upwind of the in-laws, riding to a place only she knew,
away from deadlines and familiar faces in Chesterton—
faces that remember her as she was, eyes of an angel,
unsettled, curious, fearless.

On she rode, no longer thinking about loves unknown,
she looks down at her painted fingernails, now slightly chipped,
pressing the reins, past the sandaled foot in the stirrup;
she smiles, ignoring the voices,
secure in her choices.

Her horse turns back now toward the familiar; chickens clucking, sun setting,
where the memories of her youth and the sacrifices
of her motherhood lay strewn
across the meadow, like the smell of burning of leaves,
never to leave her.

First Step

Morning routine awaits the unlucky,
having no reason to let them down
it serves a breakfast of fruit and toast,
healthy but unsatisfying,
like the last time they made love,
with predictability and fondness,
a safe, flat stone upon the ground,
never to be skipped across a pond.

Drawing Near

It's time to find you weary souls
the warmth that you once knew,
And places you would now forego
because they were untrue.

Once color-treated memories
were trimmed by someone's knife;
And hung upon the bedposts,
of someone else's life.

Chaos without remedy
stands firm against the rain,
A face that spoke a parody,
rode through the dark terrain.

The riding mare was later found
against an aging post,
Her precious saddle poorly bound,
Abandoned by her host.

Dreams that once abandoned you
return once more to send,
A silent tribute to the few
whose love would never end.

Waiting for Isabelle

A short wait filled the quiet space
as fountain fish are fed again,
Children squirm and then play chase,
while mothers shift to ease their pain.

A room is filled with unborn lives
of parents old and new,
As anxious ones with tired eyes
await a final view.

Down the hall the doctors stare
at photos of a different sort,
While smiles and nods relieve the scare,
the time we know is growing short.

The clinic door is closing soon,
the car park almost empty,
Another day has lifted gloom
and gave a gift aplenty.

Time will say nothing but I told you so
Time only knows the price we have to pay
If I could tell you, I would let you know.
—W.H. Auden, "If I Could Tell You"

Deprivation

Punishment comes with unspoken memories of two,
one who cannot recall and the other unwilling to do so.
I ask each of you who dwells in the House of the Past,
who will be left to speak of those memories that perish with the one who remembers?

That phylum of unspoken confessions will live
as long as the soul will allow, hiding like demons in delicate cocoons,
Crafted without effort, impotent, like children who no longer want to play,
depriving the still living as to their whereabouts—their authenticity.

They have everything they need to create the world.
They have only to join hands. They have only to choose.
—Campbell McGrath, "Dawn"

Confessions

A distant whimper of unspoken confessions lay tangled
amidst a bedroom filled with humidifiers and knee pillows, a creaking
ceiling fan, with the odd shaped man surrounded
now only with memories that
demanded to be spoken, to be shared,
to be freed like the cicada's final hour,
splitting his head, uncontainable, a melon vs. an ax,
he bit his hand to keep his pain silent,
memories hiding like demons in delicate cocoons,
desperate to be opened, recognized, absolved,
like the crooning cicadas, their hour is almost up,
an encroaching testament only to longevity,
the beginning of a love unfinished,
a secret untold.

If you remember me, then I don't care if everyone else forgets.
—Haruki Murakami, *Kafka on the Shore*

Passages

"Everyone is a bit scared," said the horse.
"But we are less scared together."
—Charles Mackesy, *The Boy, The Mole, The Fox and The Horse*

Dream Weavers

The women around the table stared at the symposium of yarn,
positioned around them like a house cat stretching its legs,
waiting to be touched, wound, put through a needle's eye with
aging fingers, still nimble, never wavering, welcoming the final skein
like the last dance in the gymnasiums of their youth.

The women now become the yarn's gatekeepers for its next life,
a second chance at beauty, each woman wishing she had that luxury.

Twelve Fingered Saints
"O My people, what have I done unto thee" —Micah 6:3

The gifts of St. Paul, having collapsed
upon the worshipers at Calvary Church,
came the news that the shrewd
theocracy would no longer entertain
the pilgrimage of its longstanding believers,
those that fill the pews and build the coffers and sustain
the inevitable apportionments required
under church law no longer constrained.

No votes were taken from its Sherpa-clad
advocates or mercy offered to those souls who
were discouraged from the front entrance
but instead welcomed through the Book of Discipline,
its pages worn like a love letter from the Great War,
clutched now by Twelve Fingered Saints, relentless
in their love and their hatred, creating a violent
landscape for their trail-weary travelers.

O God of Love, where is your power, relinquished
now to Houses of Worship, unadulterated
and unattended, leaving the Saints to protect The Word
instead of The Believers, offering only a Silver Hammer
to the damned, a coin in the offering plate, alleviating
the need for a Christian banner, securely offering
a final resting place for the Crown once worn
by a King adorned, now crimped into rivets.

Death in The Foyer

They say he dropped quietly, in his foyer, before he reached the door,
Blood filling his brain, slowly removing himself from his world,
An unexpected interruption, untimely and unannounced,
He was no longer in charge, separated from his briefcase for the final time.

Passing now through stages that made him who he was and who he would become
Disbelieving it could be the end and then quickly accepting it (as though choice were involved)
His final thoughts were of wives and children and lovers unknown
Thoughts that he will share now only with himself.

Willing but unable to speak, his imprisoned final words were
Never to be spoken, smothered by the shutdown of his main engine.
Were those sirens in the distance or a ringing deep inside?
He was in the process of checking out, barely aware of his
surroundings, except for the red rug.

Grasping for his wife's hand, he is unable to squeeze it,
Only to feel her long, warm fingers, protecting now what no longer needs protecting
And to hear her soft, fading pleas, while she moved in slow-motion across
A landscape of windows and family photos and plant stands and a new television.

He was to die upon a rug he used to vacuum and had admired from a distance.
Now he becomes part of its fabric, his soul moving toward a new life
Less worldly than the one which at that instant he was leaving,
But a new life just the same.

Speed Bumps
for DMGA

There was nothing to do but watch her,
moving awkwardly toward the car, her knees bandaged,
glasses slipping, back bent toward the pavement.
The emergency brake was stuck, the wipers erratic.

Pulling out carefully, then accelerating through
the speed bumps for the third time this day,
her mind focused on only one thing—doing that one thing now,
not tomorrow or Tuesday and certainly not until the children
could come to help.

Demonstrating to angry motorists everywhere
there is nothing so unpredictable as a 92-year-old widow
racing across the divided highways of her mind,
with nothing left to lose except being unable to do the same
thing tomorrow, an eternity to her now as she pulls into
the intersection of What Would You Do and Help Me Jesus.

Summer Evenings

"Anyway, I keep picturing all these little kids playing some game in this big field of rye and all. Thousands of little kids, and nobody's around—nobody big, I mean—except me. And I'm standing on the edge of some crazy cliff. What I have to do, I have to catch everybody if they start to go over the cliff—I mean if they're running and they don't look where they're going I have to come out from somewhere and catch them. That's all I do all day. I'd just be the catcher in the rye and all. I know it's crazy, but that's the only thing I'd really like to be."
—J.D. Salinger, *A Catcher in the Rye*

Turning Away from Sarah McLachlan
"Rudeness is the weak man's imitation of strength."
—Edmund Burke

Backs turned against the stage, glasses lifted
high, passing the blackened salmon on fine china,
opening their monogrammed silk napkins,
jammed into the center ring, paying no attention
to what unfolded behind them, casually inattentive,
like an unhurried cancer nurse
whose patient would not know the
difference.

On they drank, mouths moving, lips
snarling, crowing into the night, a dark
murmur against a bright voice, their
backs still turned against the stage, the performer
sang on, unimpeded by the cacophonous
guests, whose glass fruit cups and
Cakebread Cabernet were emptied into their
lonely hearts, who casually listened as though
they were on their north Fulton decks listening
to their iTunes instead of to this live angel
just 50 feet away.

On she sang, against the clanging of chairs,
the grinning rich, the corn salad crowd, who
were not going to be denied their dinner table
conversation, even in the midst of this most
virtuous voice of many octaves, melodious, soothing,
defying the storm clouds, sweeping away from the
disorderly with her songs and her sweaty blouse
and tight jeans, reduced now to a piano bar singer.

Candles lined the inner circle, like tables in a bull ring
without the bull, but with plenty of red tablecloths
and strident groups of six, some family, some friends,
all undeterred, uninterrupted, unaware of

their surroundings, dispassionately musing just
loudly enough for two rows up to hear, about their
little day and their important lives and the disappointing
saltiness of their catered chicken salad.

A final bow against the clicks of wine glasses
and coiffed, middle aged men in nipple-soaked golf shirts,
the performer thanked the crowd, but thought how nice
it might have been to sing *I Will Remember You*
to a venue where thousands might come
to hear only the music, though knowing
all the while that this place was special, and
that the inner circle of silverware and candelabras
and retirees were the night's only true center stage,
she waved goodbye and walked briskly away.

Guard Duty

He had climbed the barbed wire
once before, while the old
man slept in his cabin and his son
sat outside grinning at a smoldering
fire, a shotgun across his
knee, a silent sentry protecting
no one, watching embers
attempt to thrive back to fire.
This time
neighbors heard
the shotgun's blast cracked
once, then
in darkness, searing
the prowler's shirt
while the cabin lights
remained dark.
I cross the meadow, my life
throbbing red through my fingers.

Who is Listening?

Downstairs
I hear the muted laughter
of young adults
and upstairs the cries
of children that pierce
the ear, a trumpeter's
call that neighbors
ignore and that sunrise
will not silence.

The Whistler

The Whistler bagged groceries six days a week,
whistling a familiar but unknown tune as he pushed noisy carts
for people he did not know but always recognized,
unable to accept tips, he whistled perfectly, like Bing Crosby, often in
   the rain,
with strong, dark arms, dressed in a yellow windbreaker,
estranged from his only son but bonded now with bag-toting
   strangers,
dutifully collecting carts so rudely left strewn across the parking lot.
He clocked out that Saturday night and bought a lottery ticket on the
   way home,
returning to work the next day, still whistling, three million dollars
   richer.

David R. Altman, an Ohio native who resides in Hoschton, Georgia, was nominated for Georgia Author of the Year for his 2014 chapbook, *Death in the Foyer* (Finishing Line Press). His poem "Picking Up My Crying Father at the Airport" was published in the July 2017 edition of the *American Journal of Poetry* and his poem "Turning Away from Sarah McLachlan" was published in the December 2017 edition of the *Blue Mountain Review*. His poem "Cold Remembered" was published in the Riza Press' *Multimedia Poetry and Art Journal* in January 2020.

Altman, 70, is a columnist for MainStreet News, Inc. which operates five weekly newspapers serving northeast Georgia. He has been married for 48 years to his high school sweetheart, Lisa Roberts Altman. They have three grown daughters and seven grandkids. Altman is currently working on a third collection of poems and a memoir.

He can be reached at altmandavidr@gmail.com or through his website at www.davidraltman.com.

www.ingramcontent.com/pod-product-compliance
Lightning Source LLC
Chambersburg PA
CBHW022124090426
42743CB00008B/992